I0505276

AI DRAGON & LANDSCAPE COLORING BOOK

Hey there, I'm Jeremy Hubert Burt. I was feeling inspired and decided to use a prompt to create some 3D coloring book pages. The prompt I used was:

"Create a 3D coloring book page featuring a contour architectural style. The design should also include elements such as a dragon, trap, spider web, and other haunting and horror elements to make it more exciting for coloring enthusiasts. The goal is to create a visually striking and captivating maze design that will engage and entertain coloring book users. black and white only. more contrast."

After creating the design, I decided to edit the levels in GIMP in greyscale image mode to give it that extra touch of depth and detail. The whole process only took me a day, and I'm really happy with the results. I even published the pages using the Sqribble ebook maker, which was super easy to use. Check out the link if you want to Publish Your eBook: https://bit.ly/3nVzjvK.

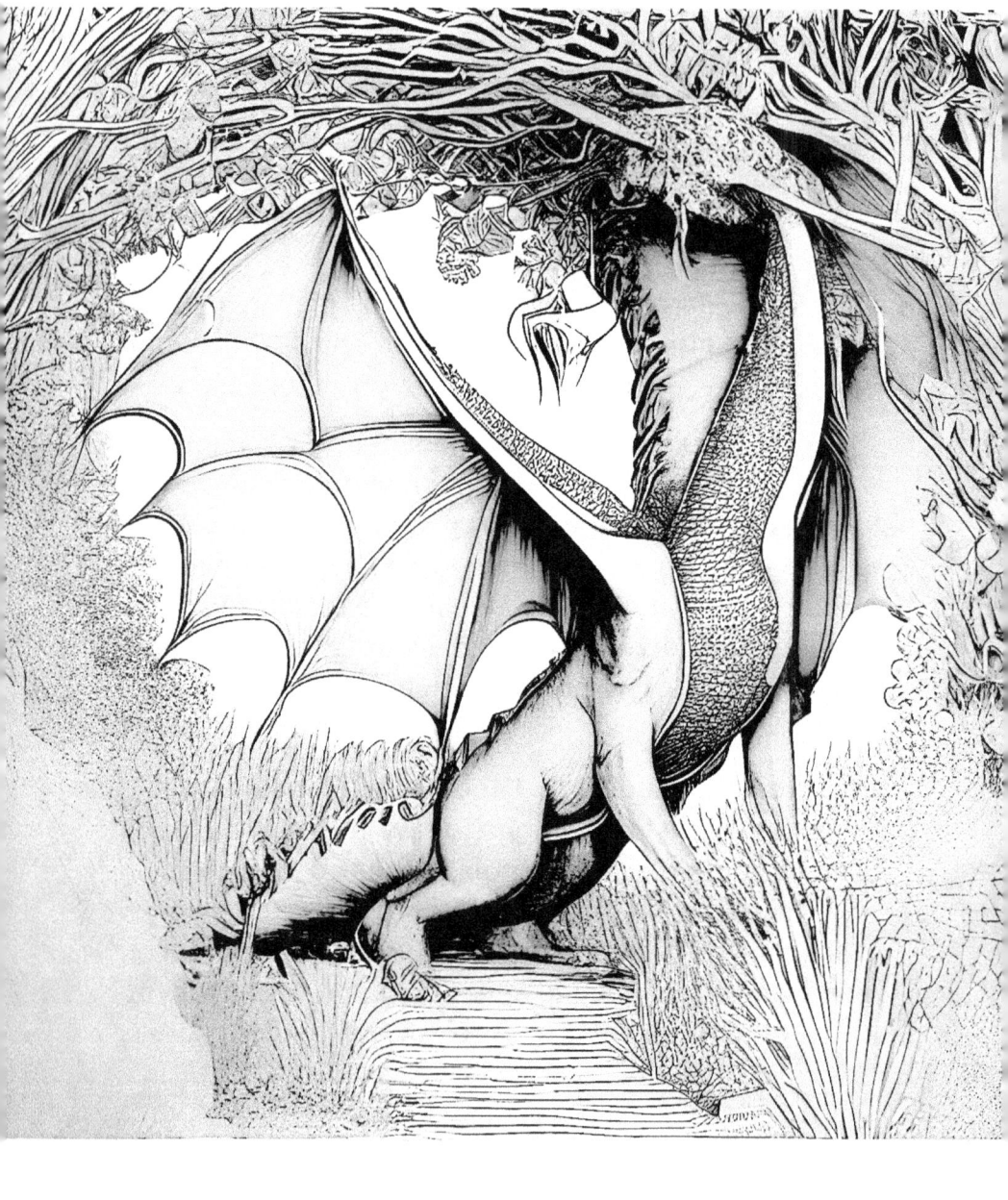

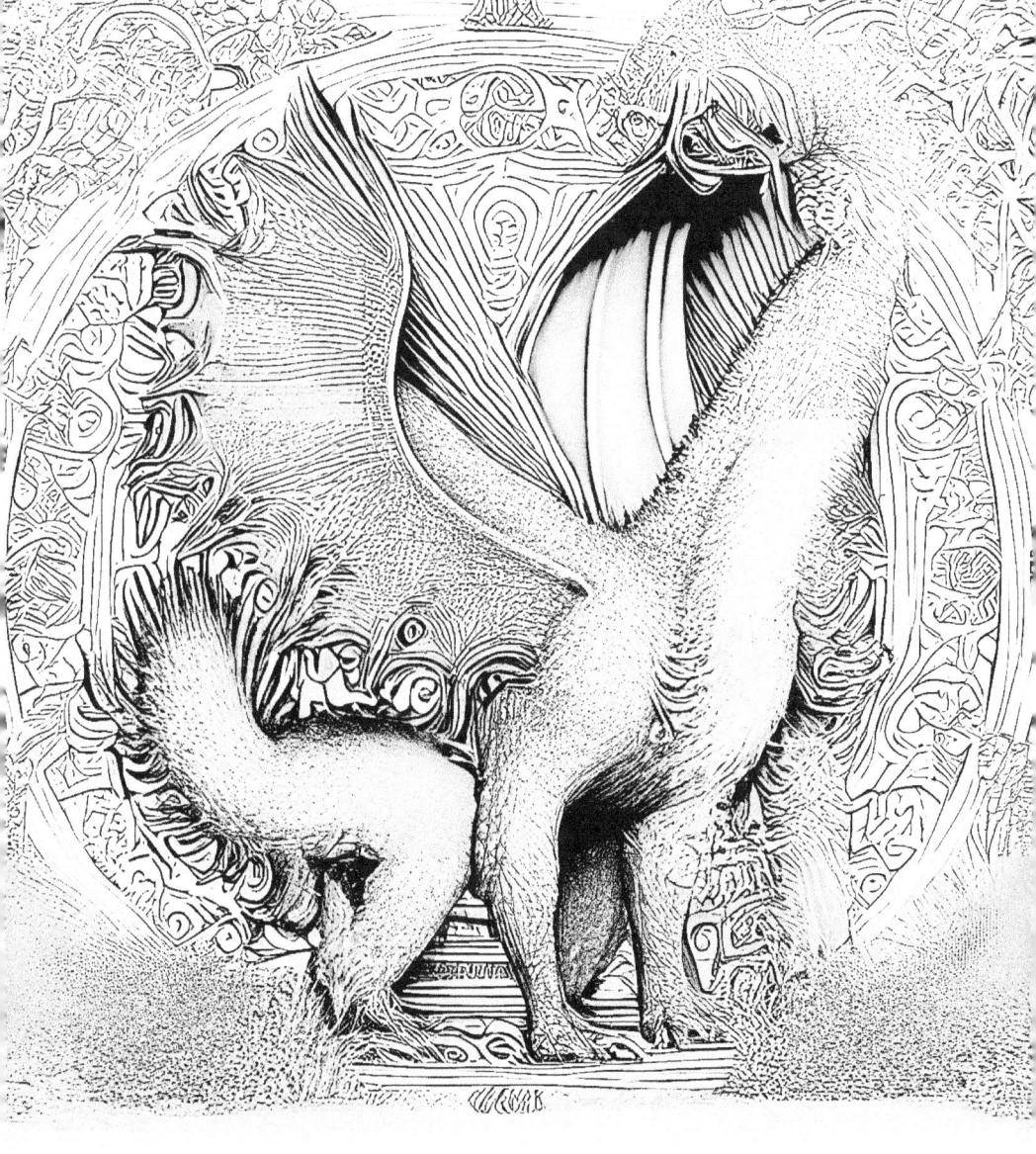

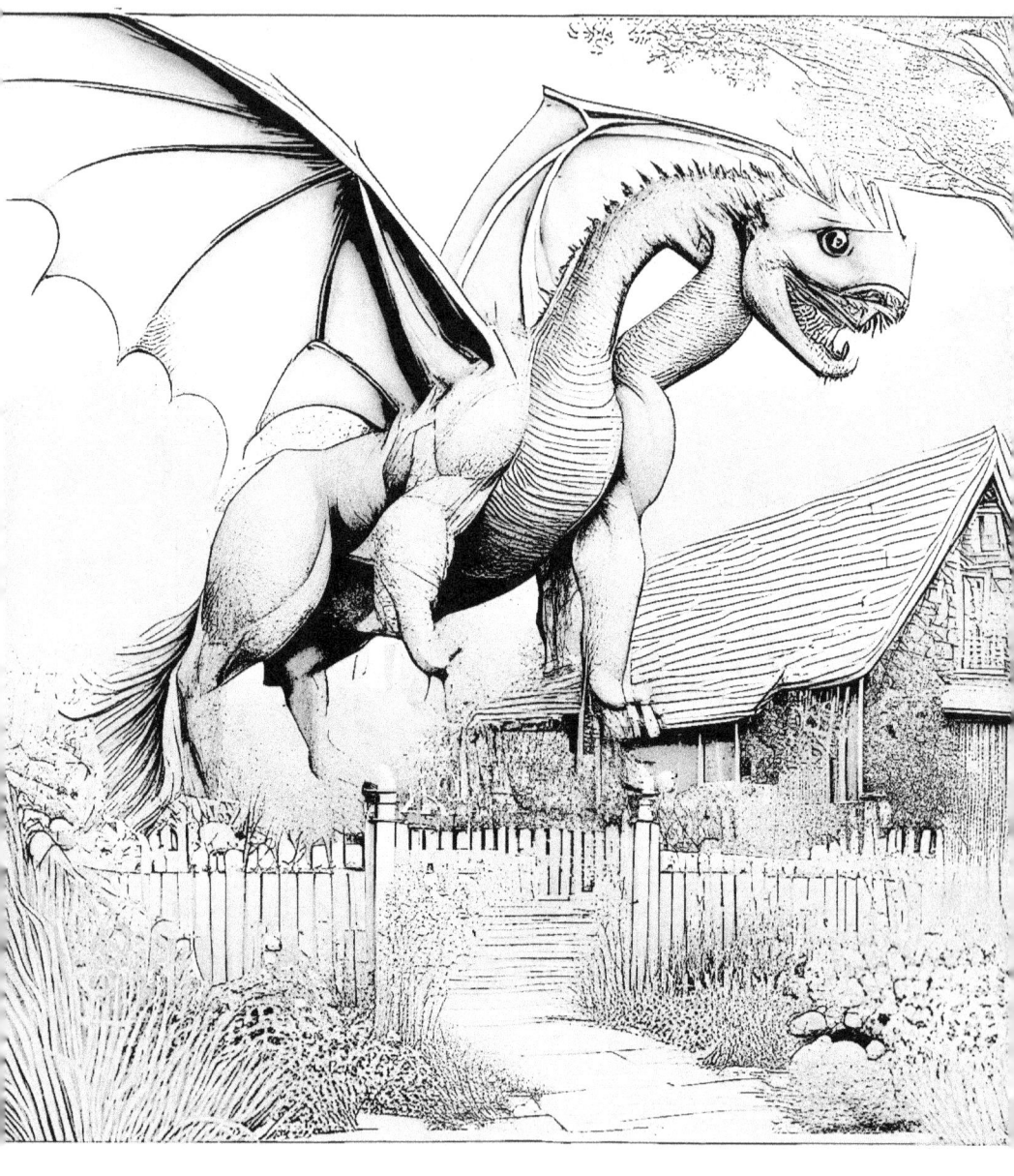

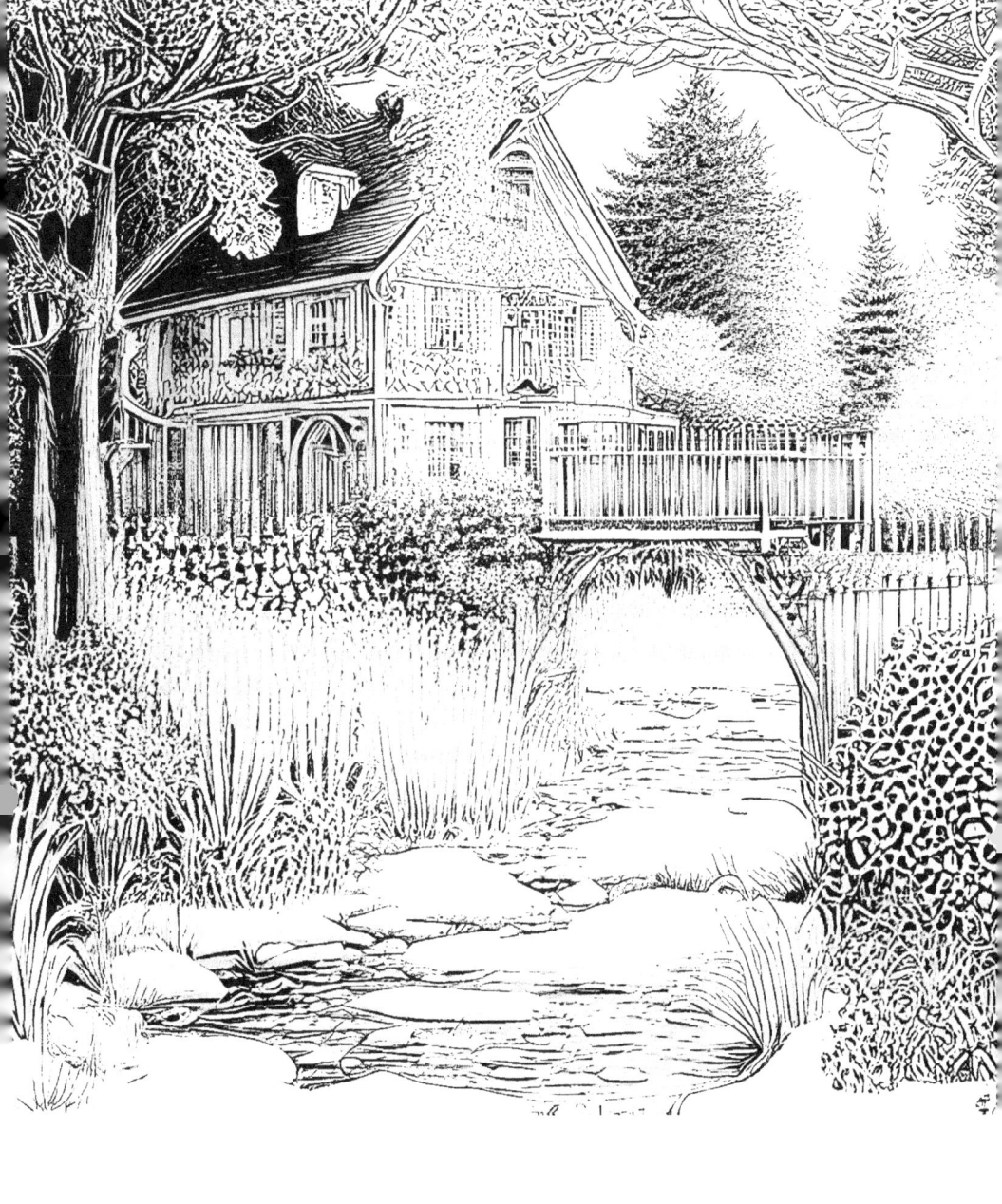

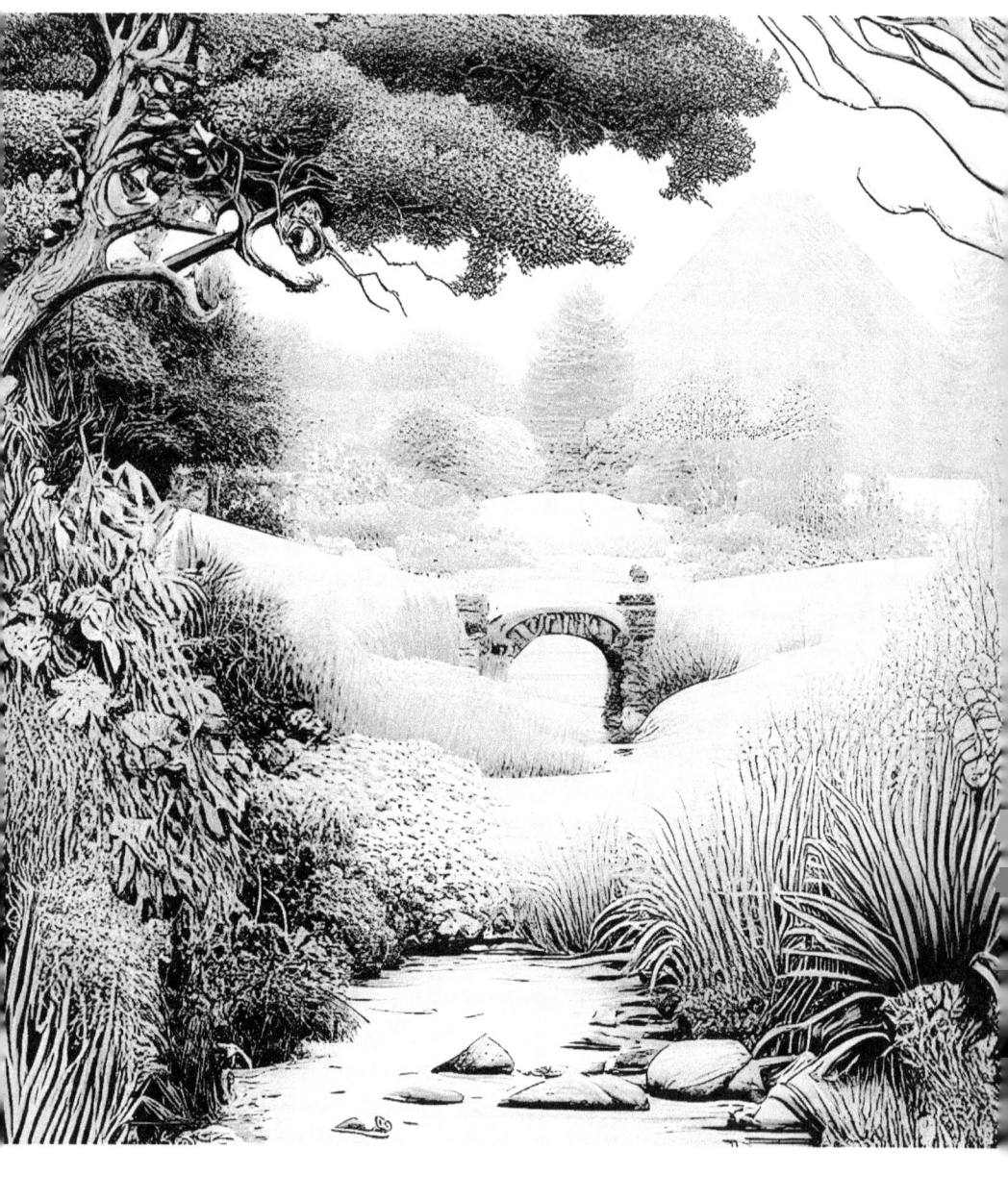

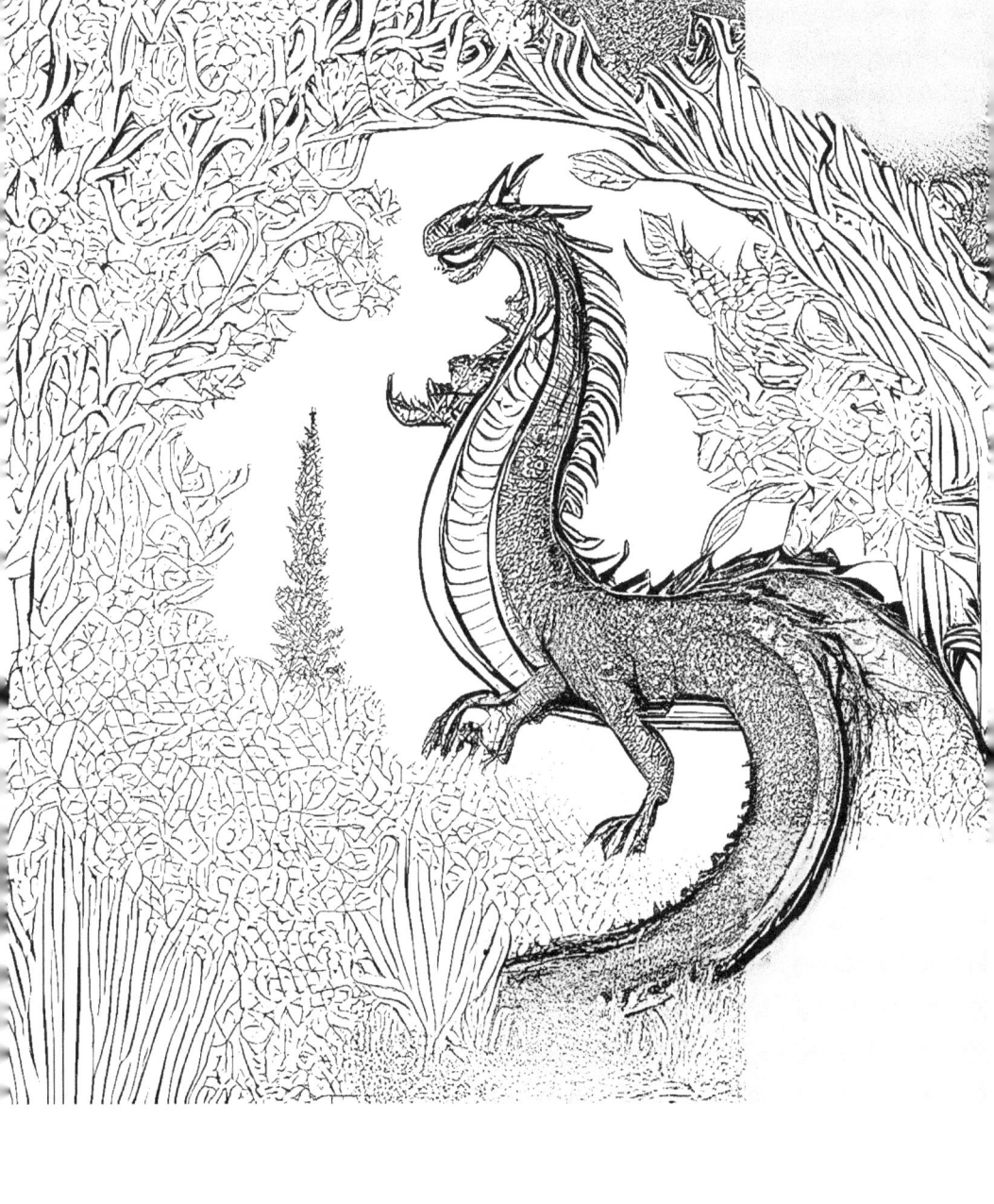

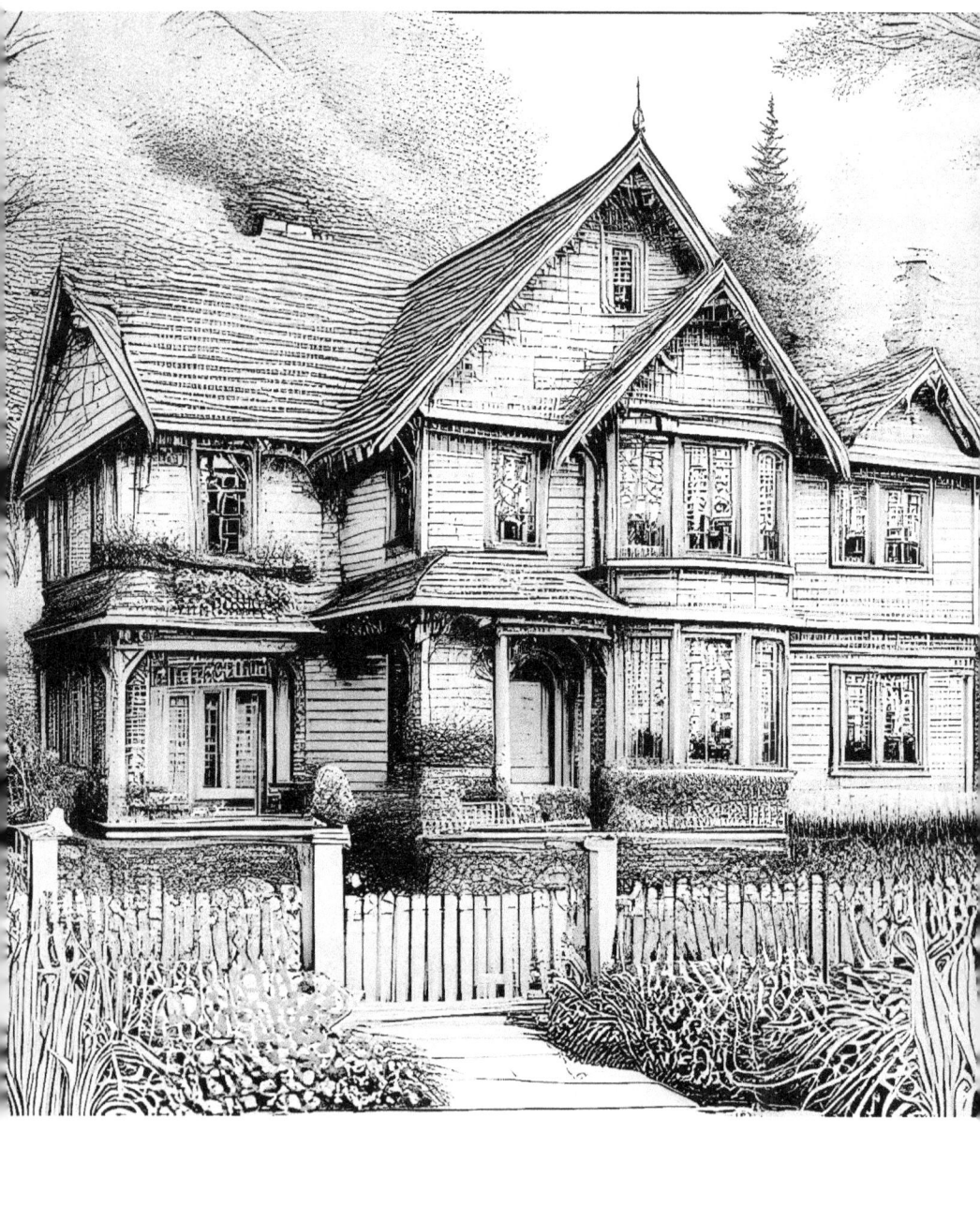

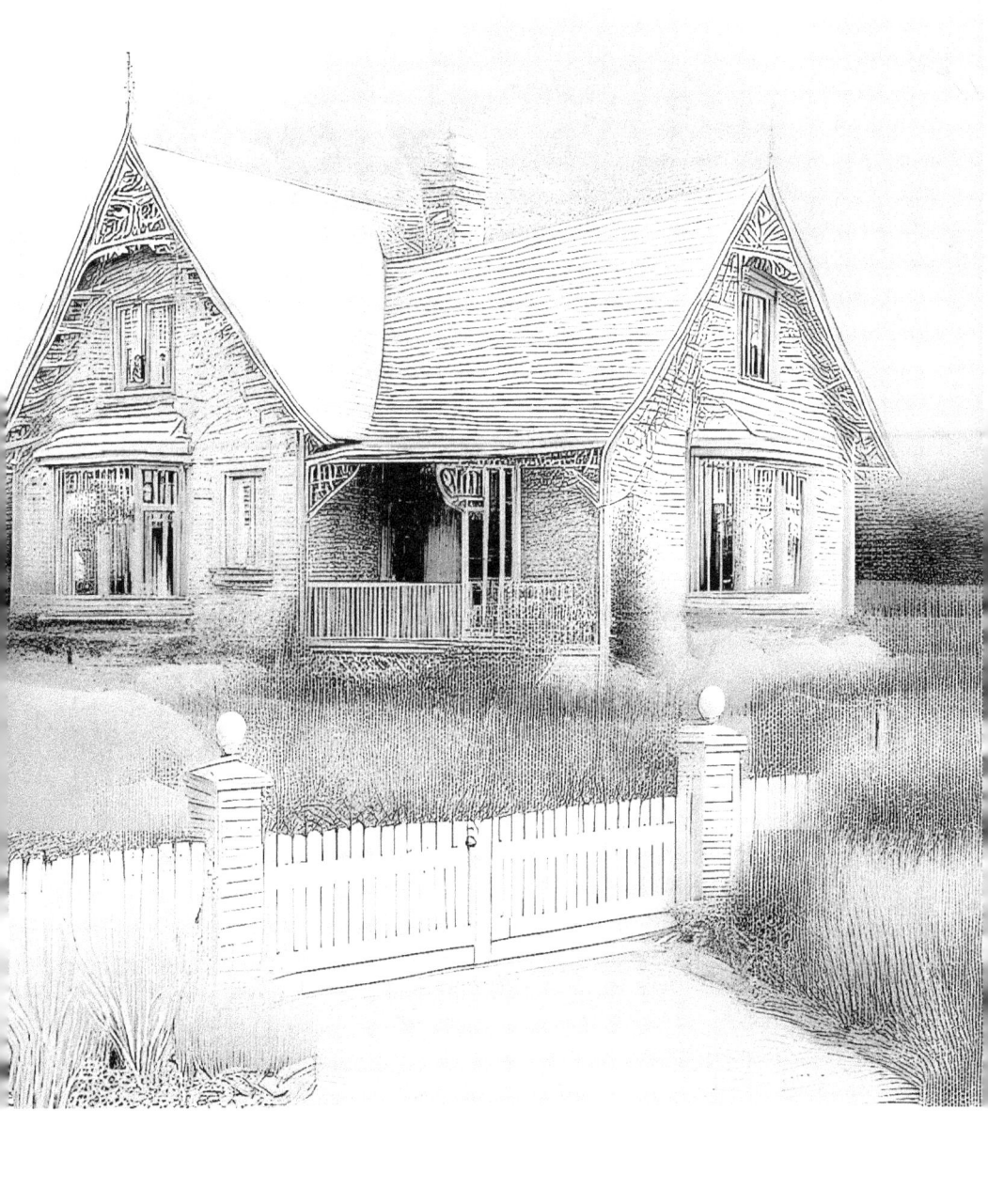

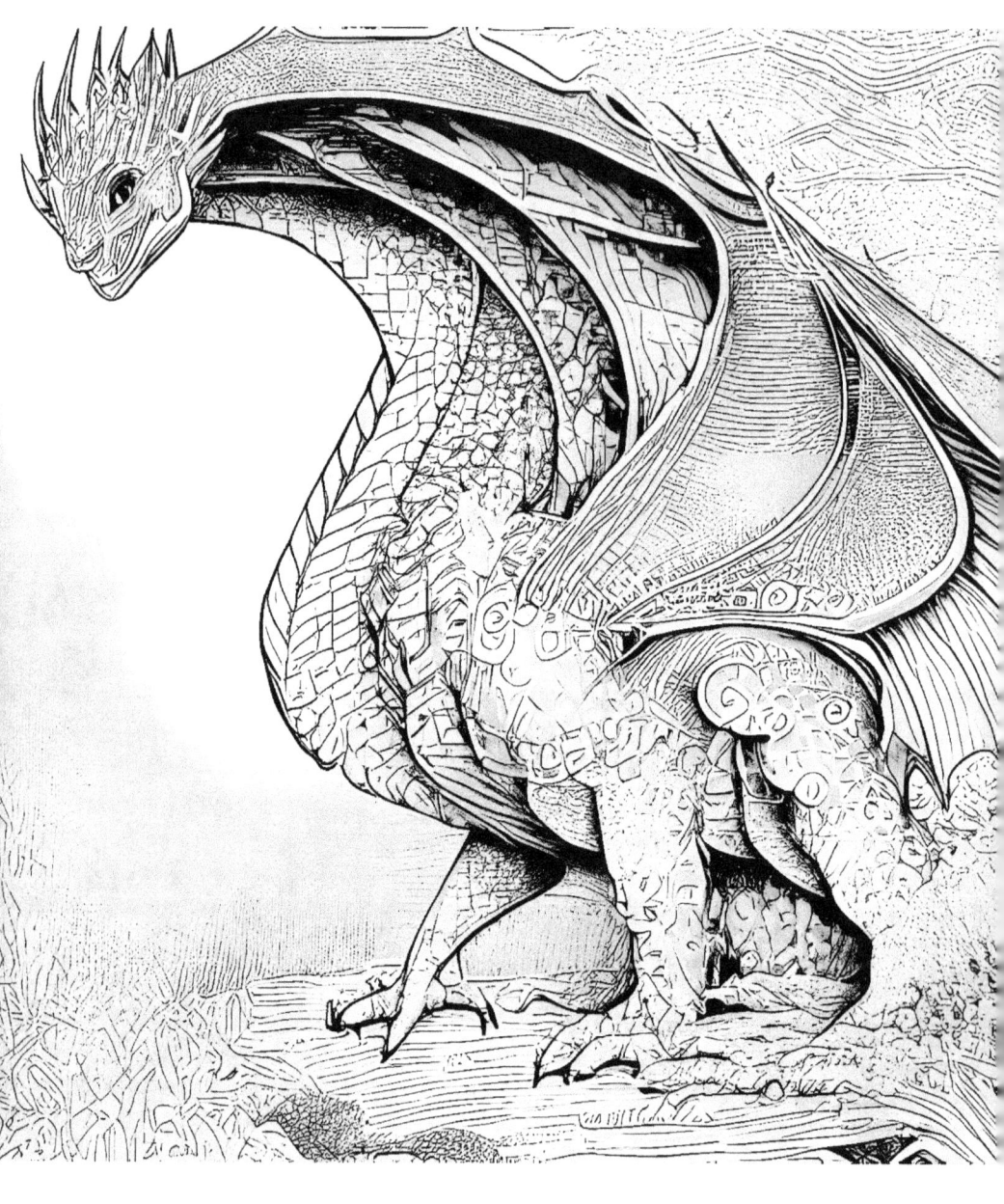

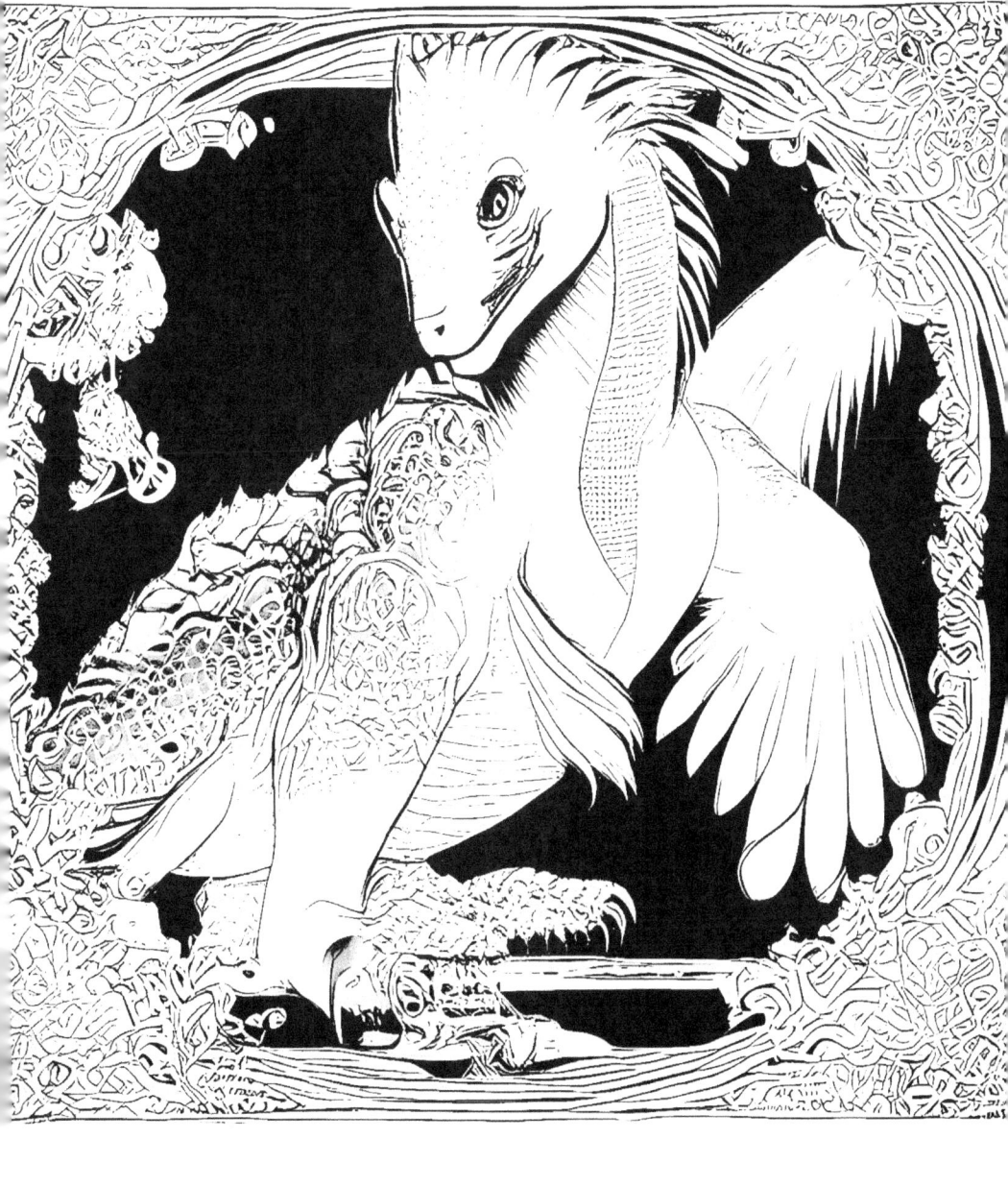

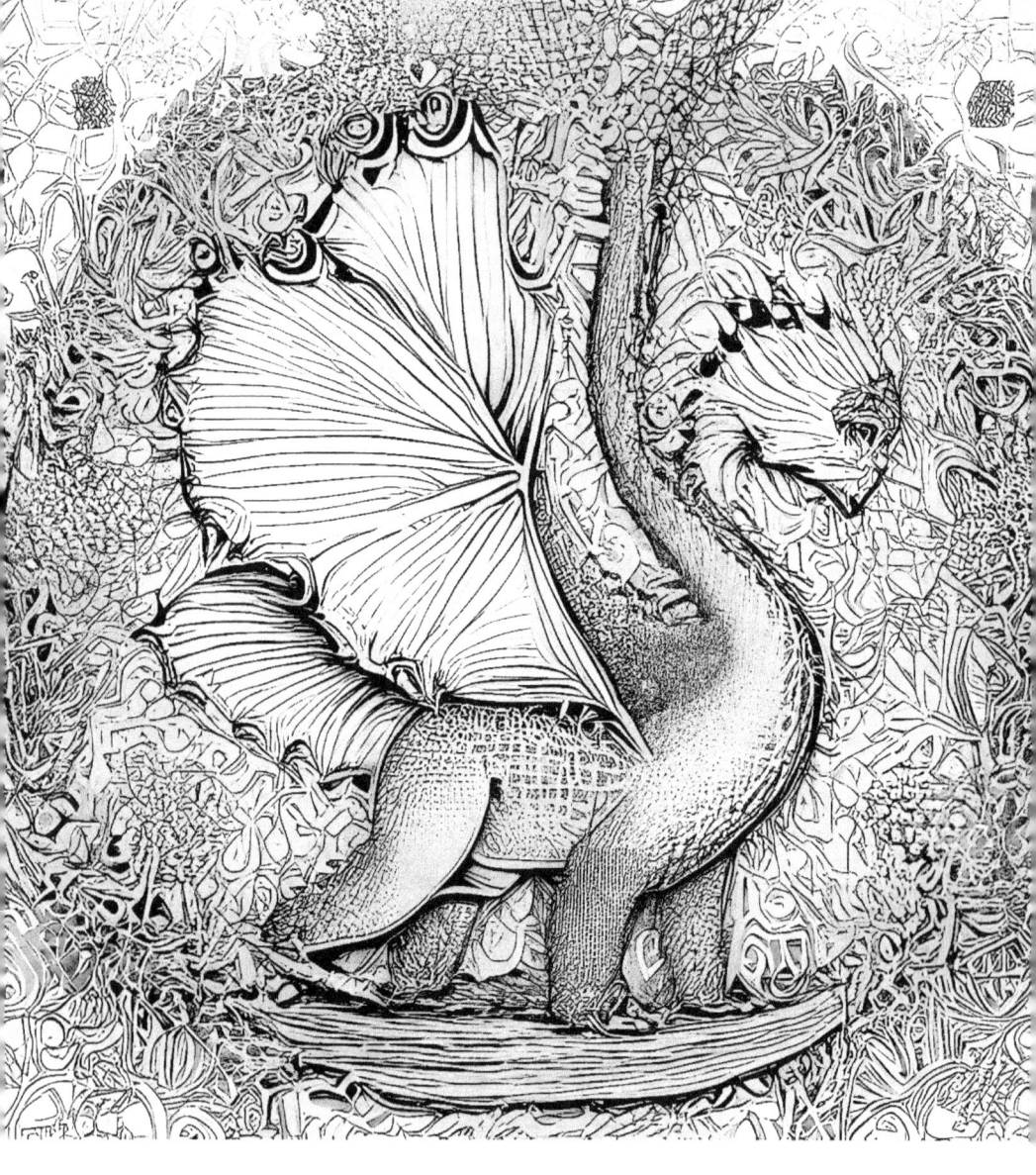

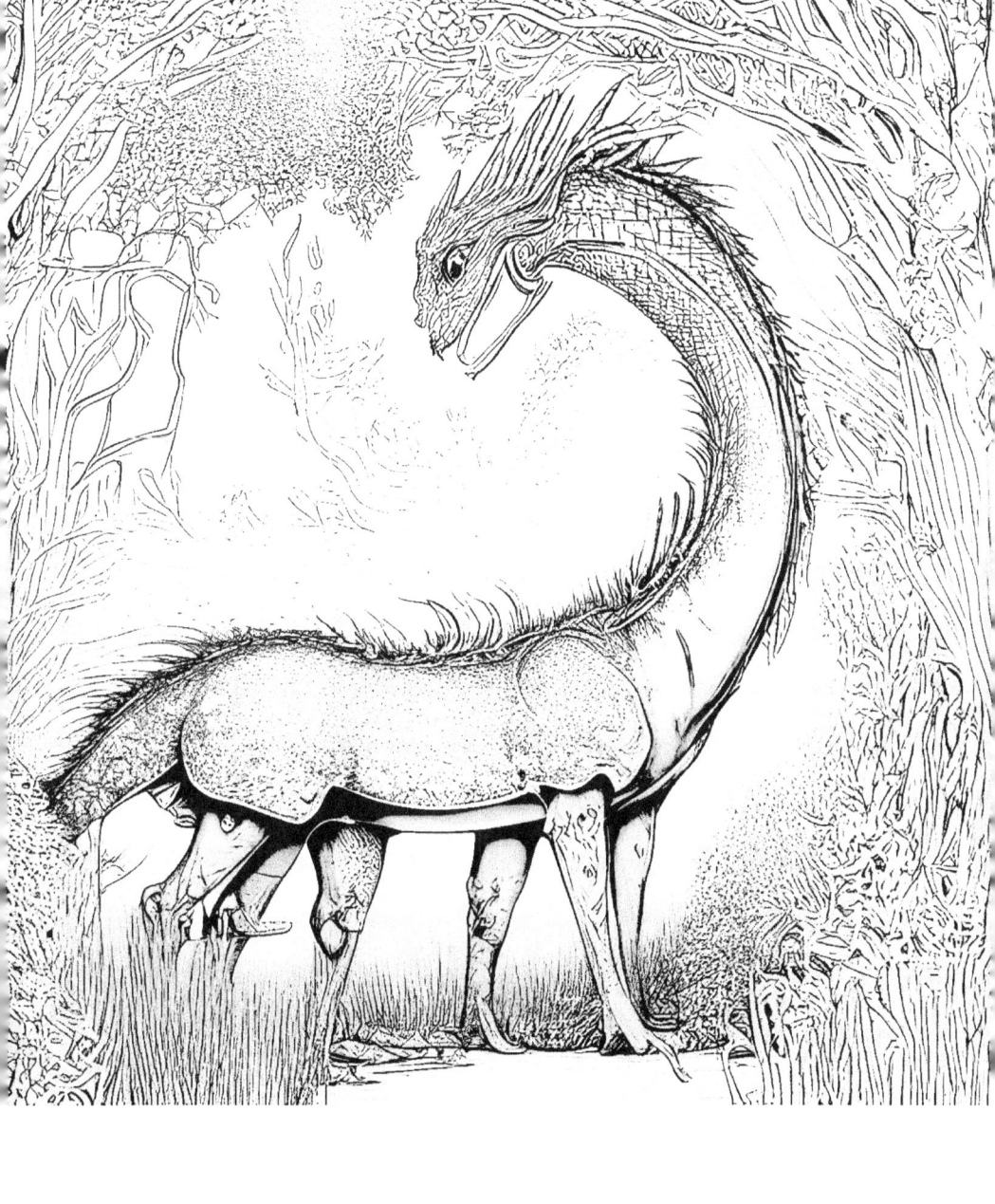

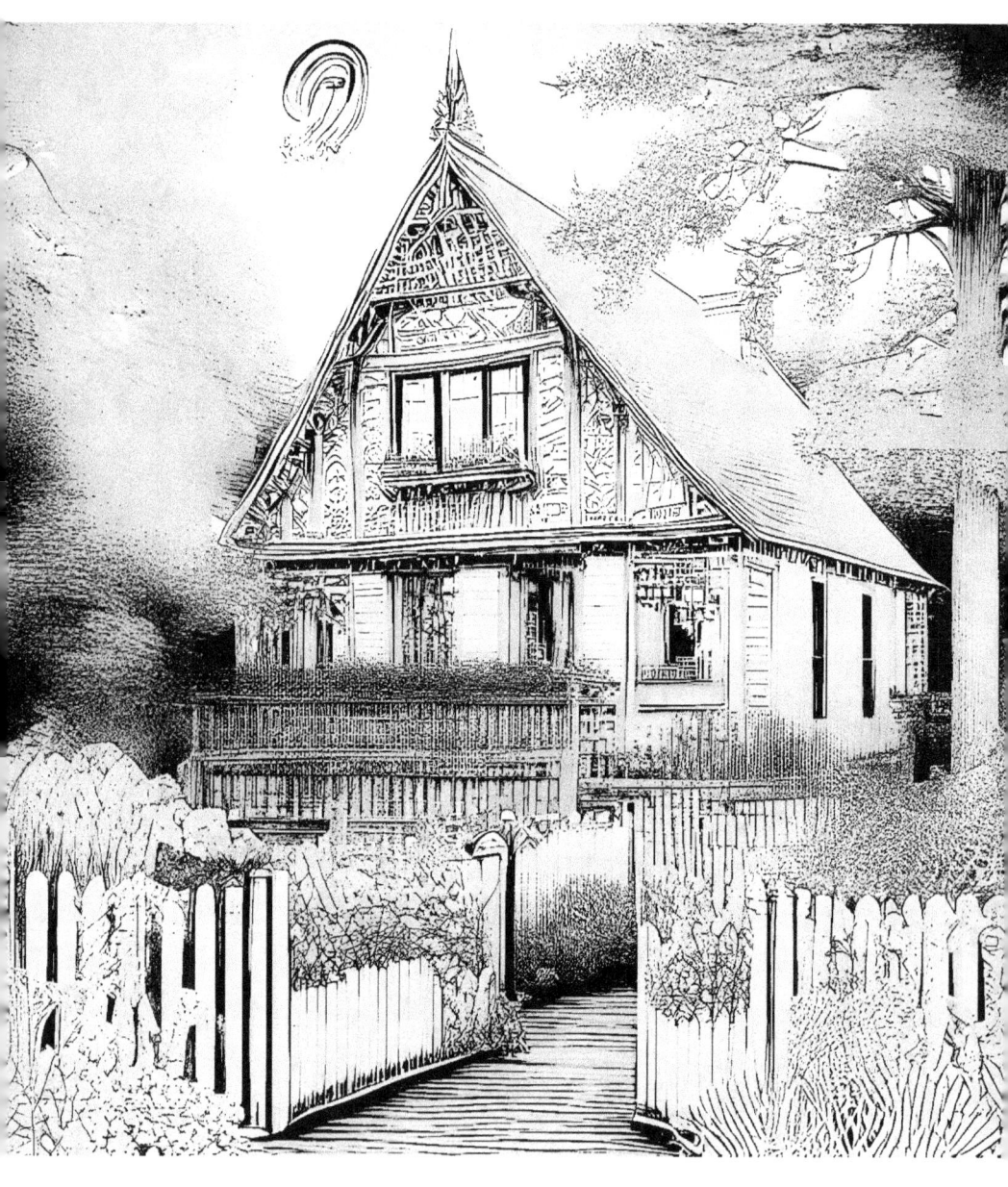

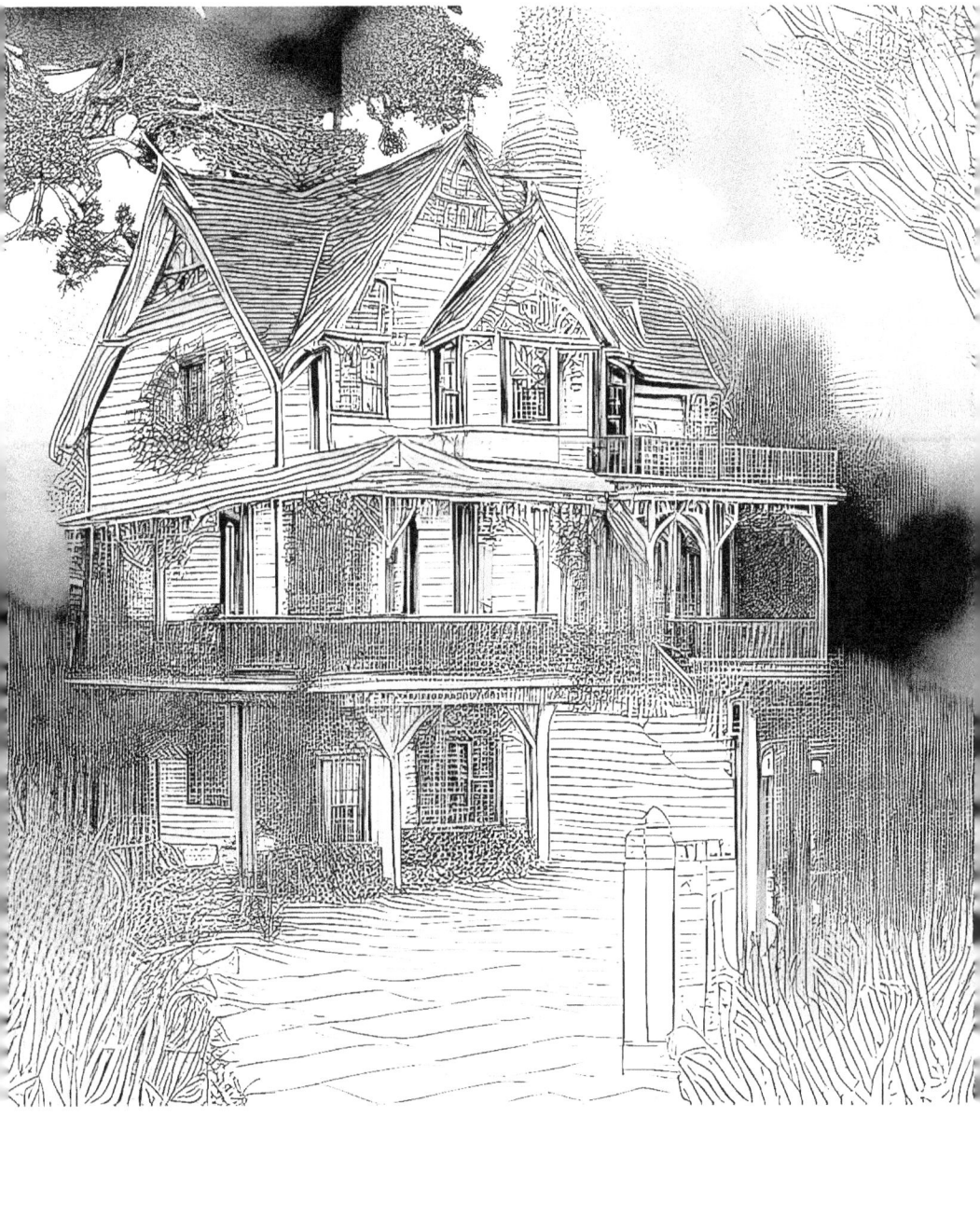

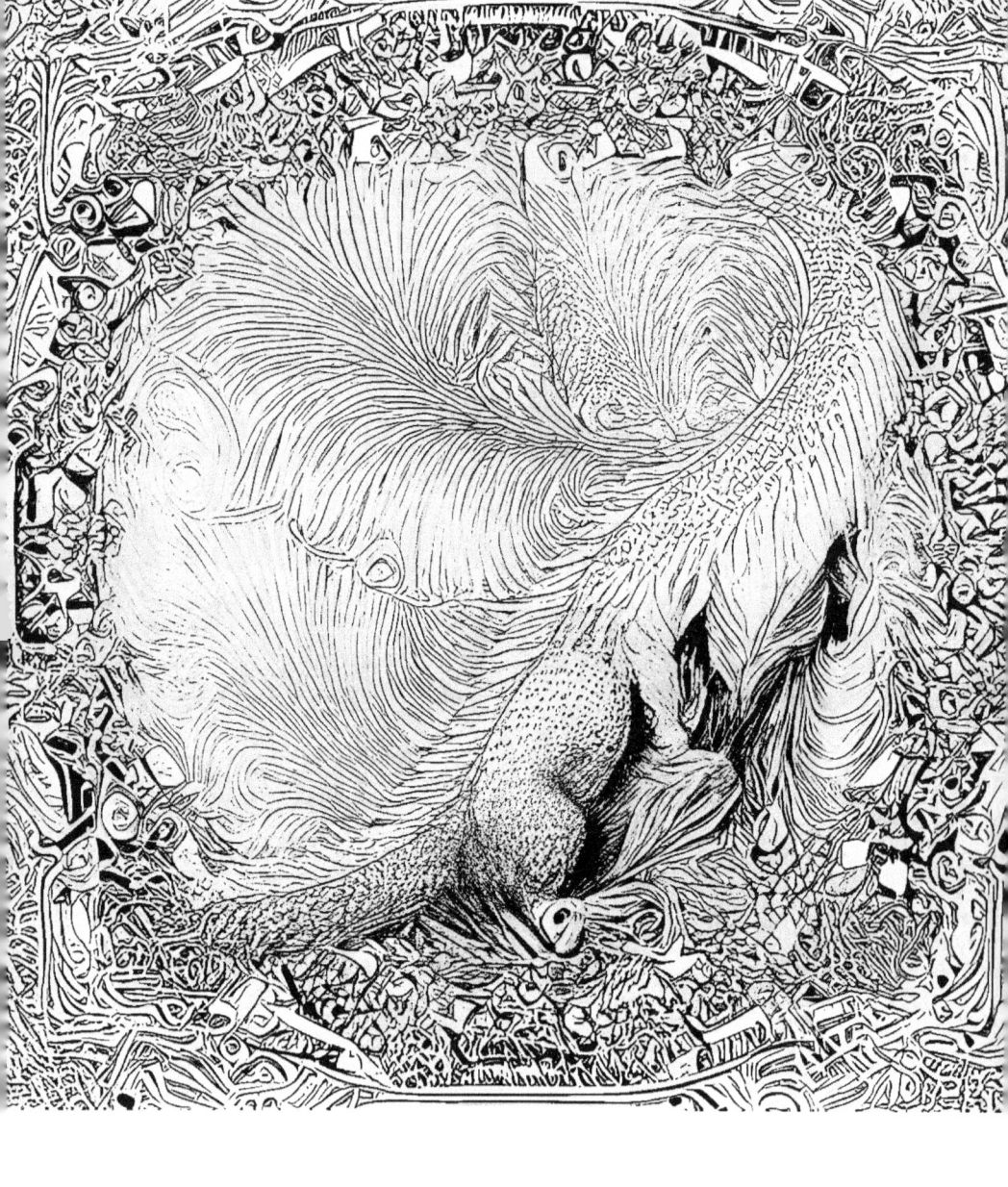

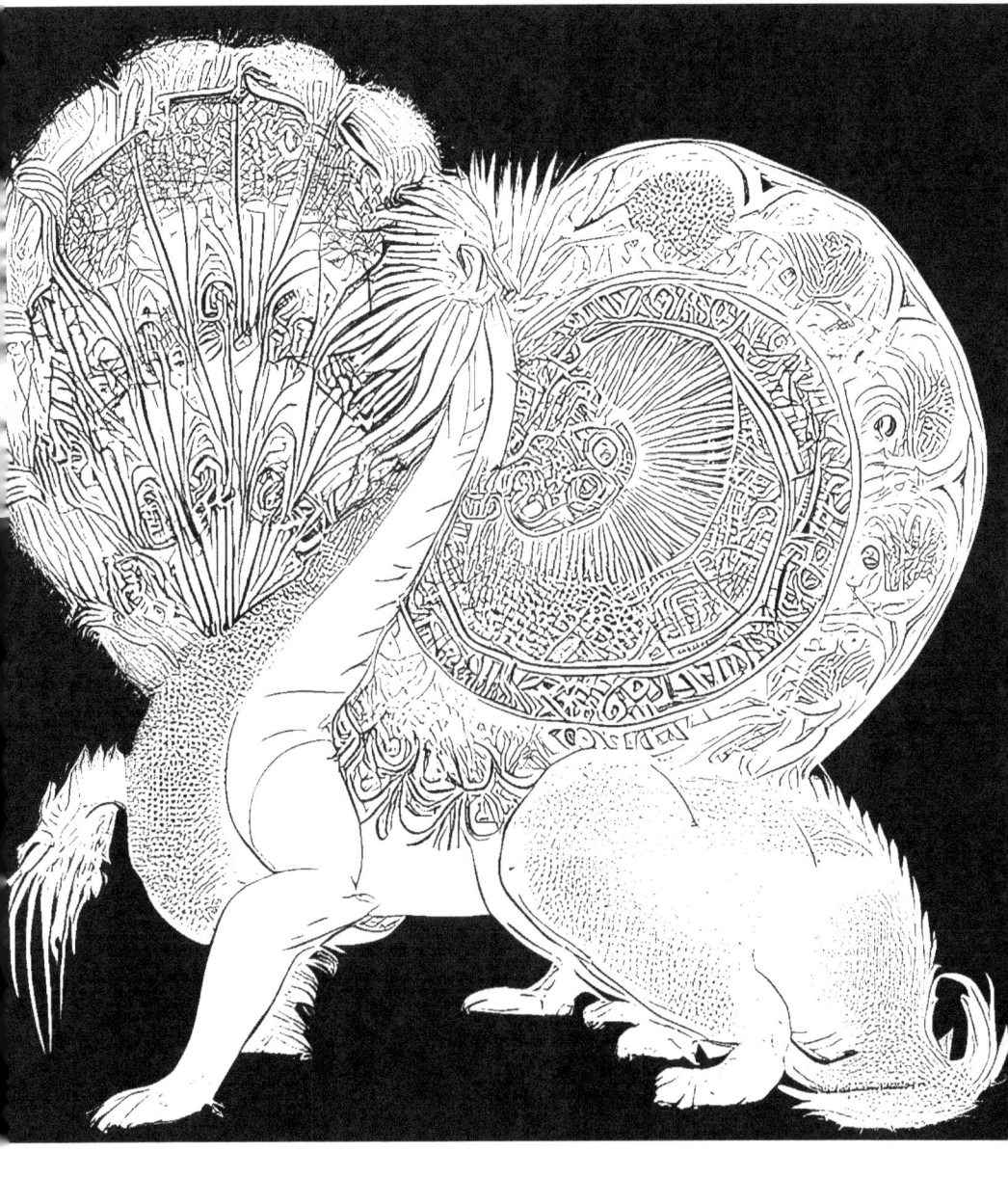

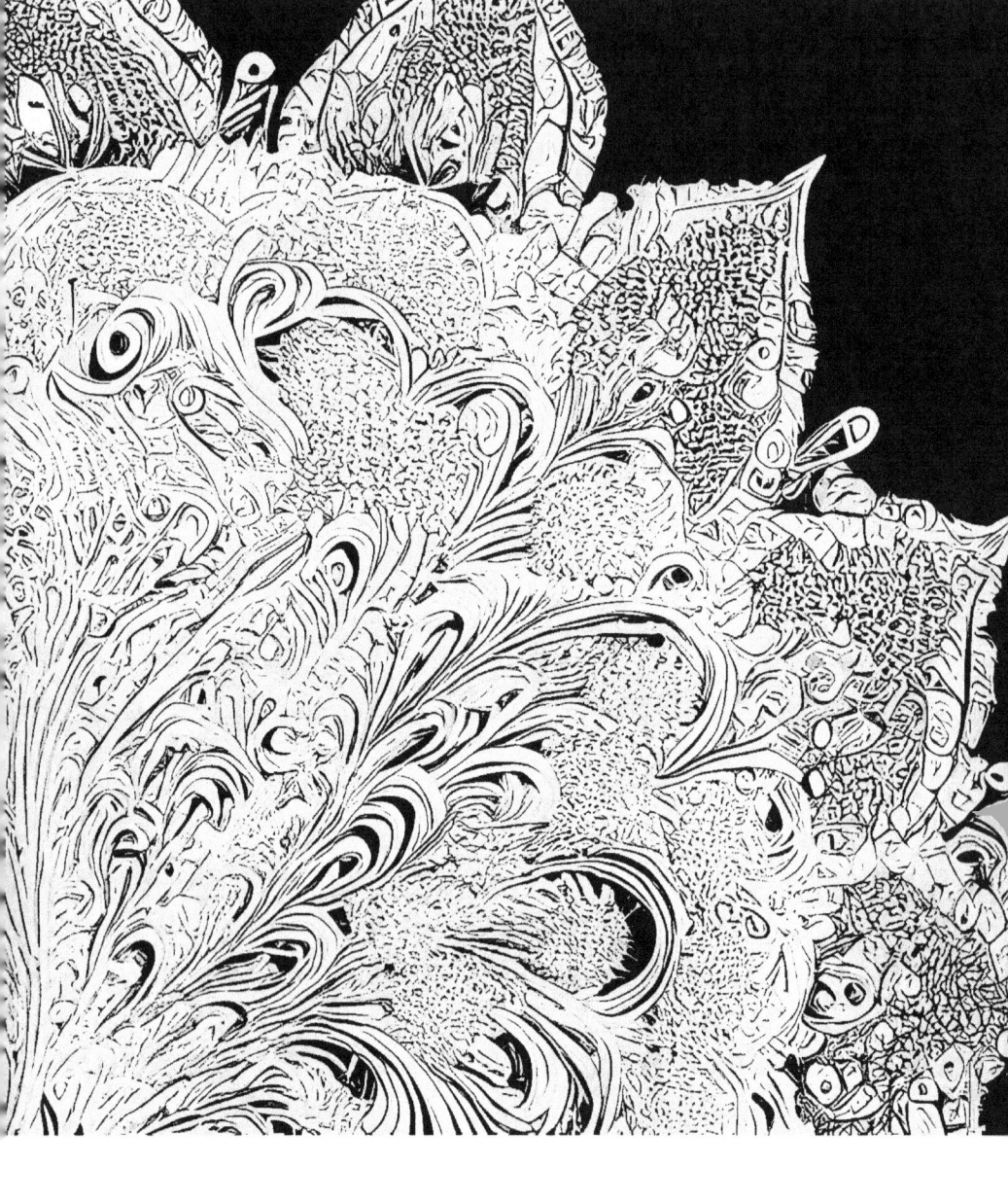

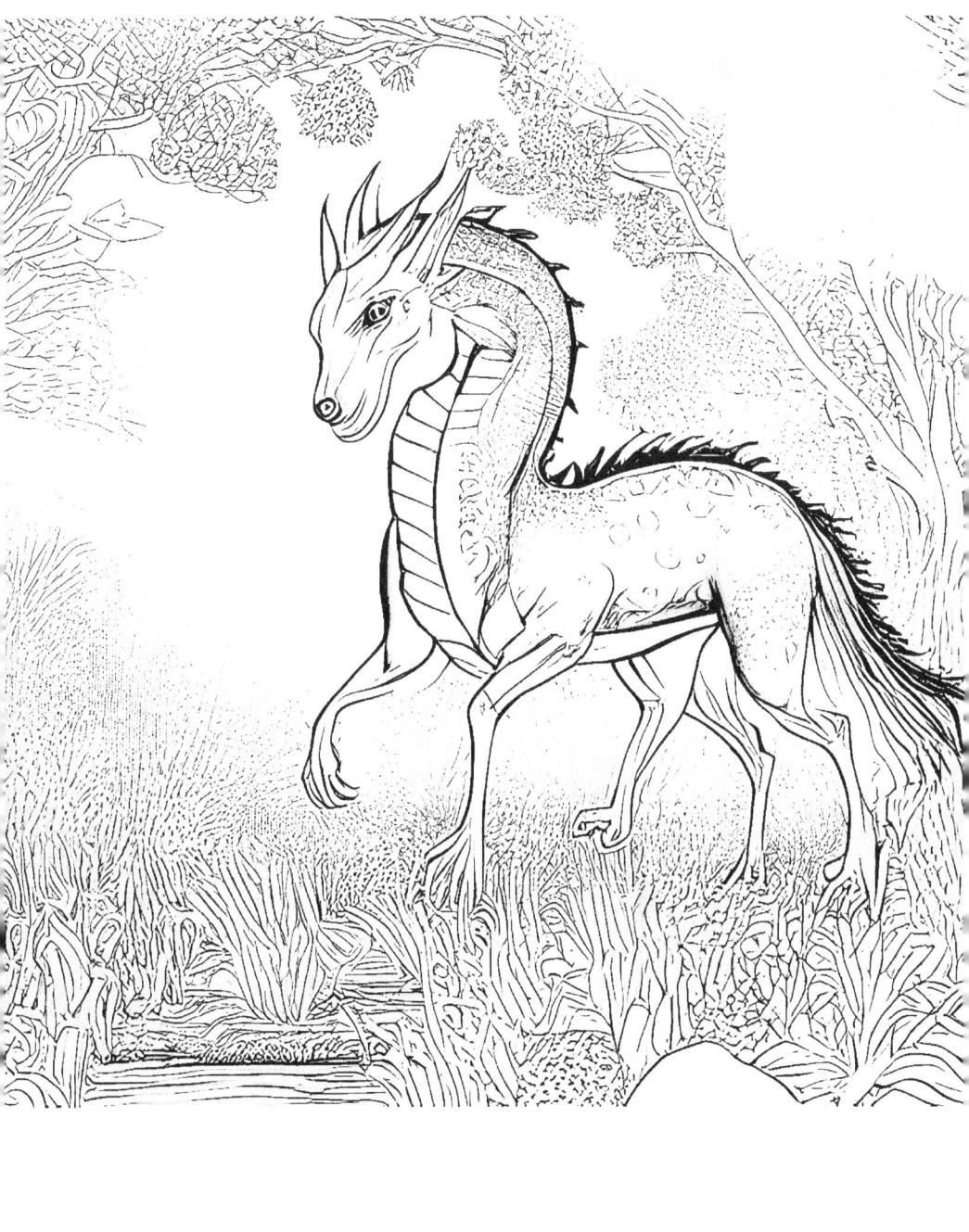

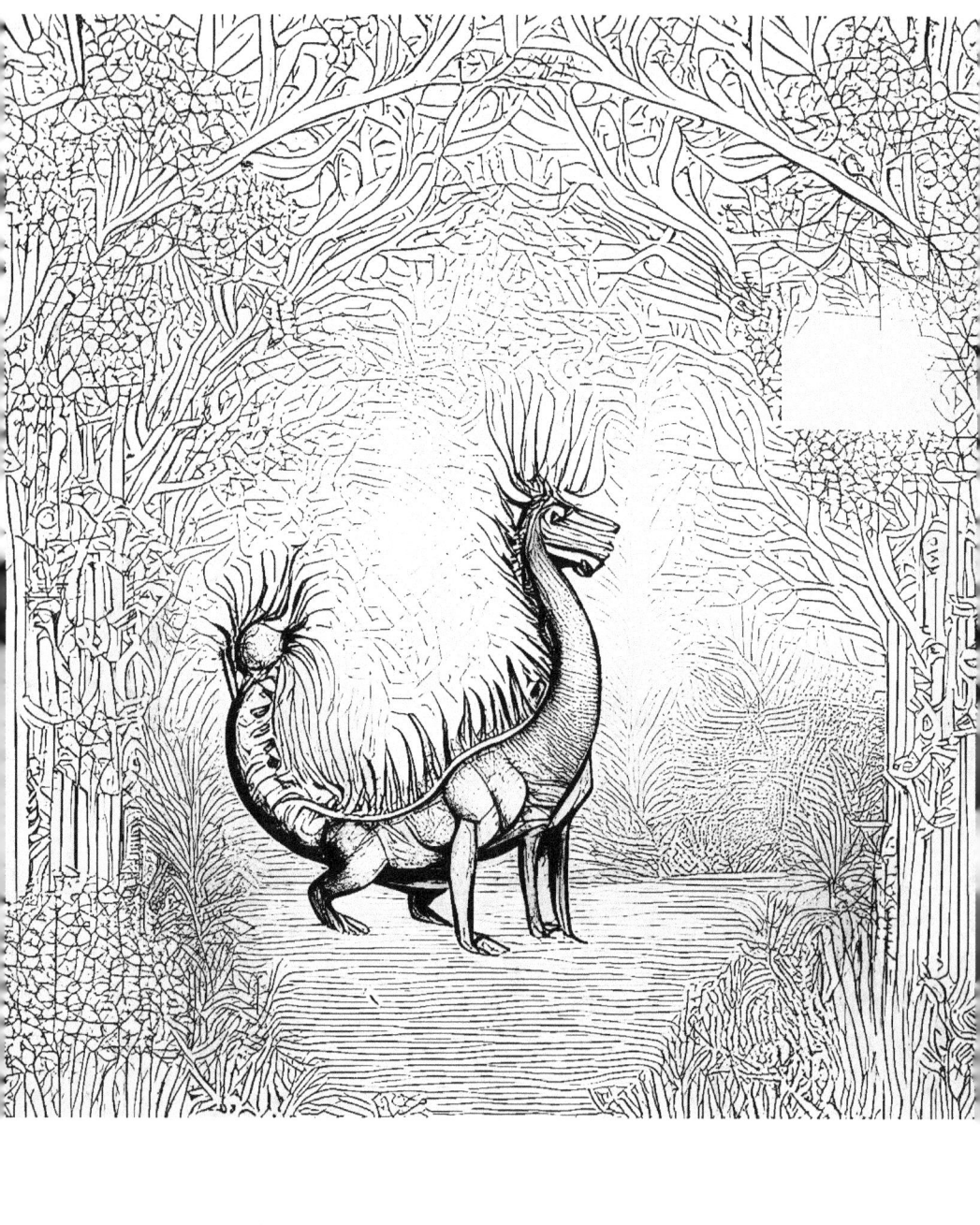

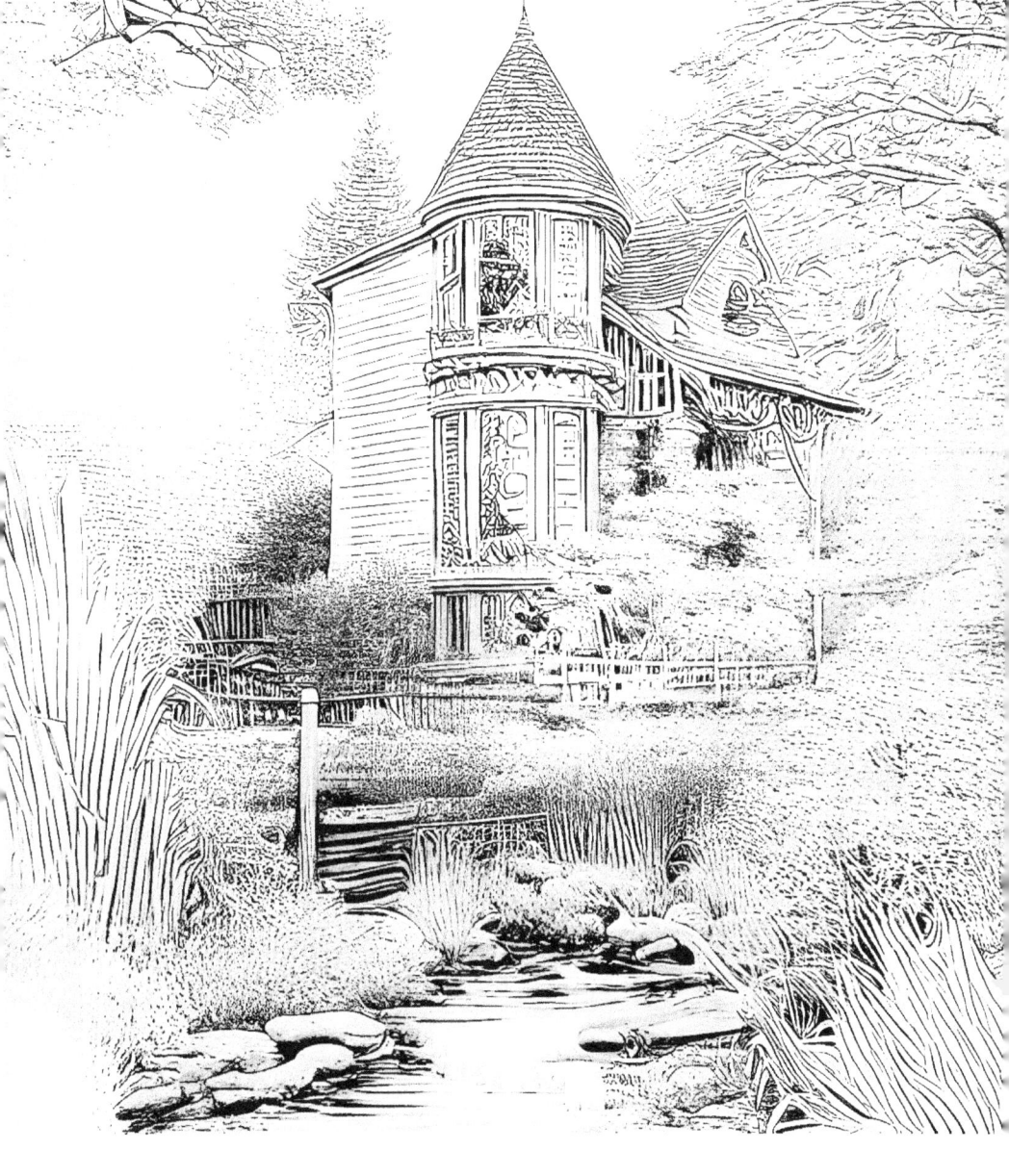

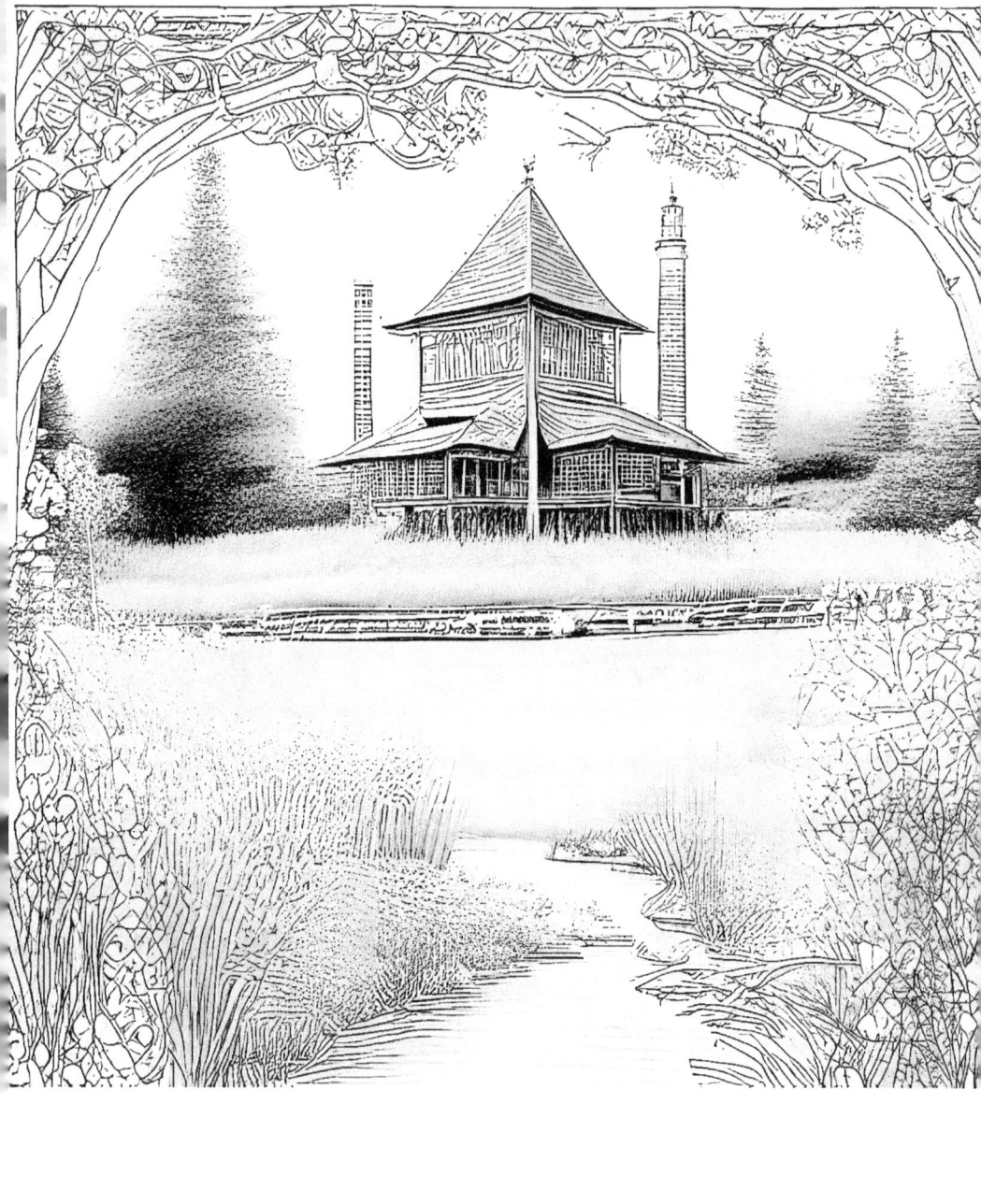

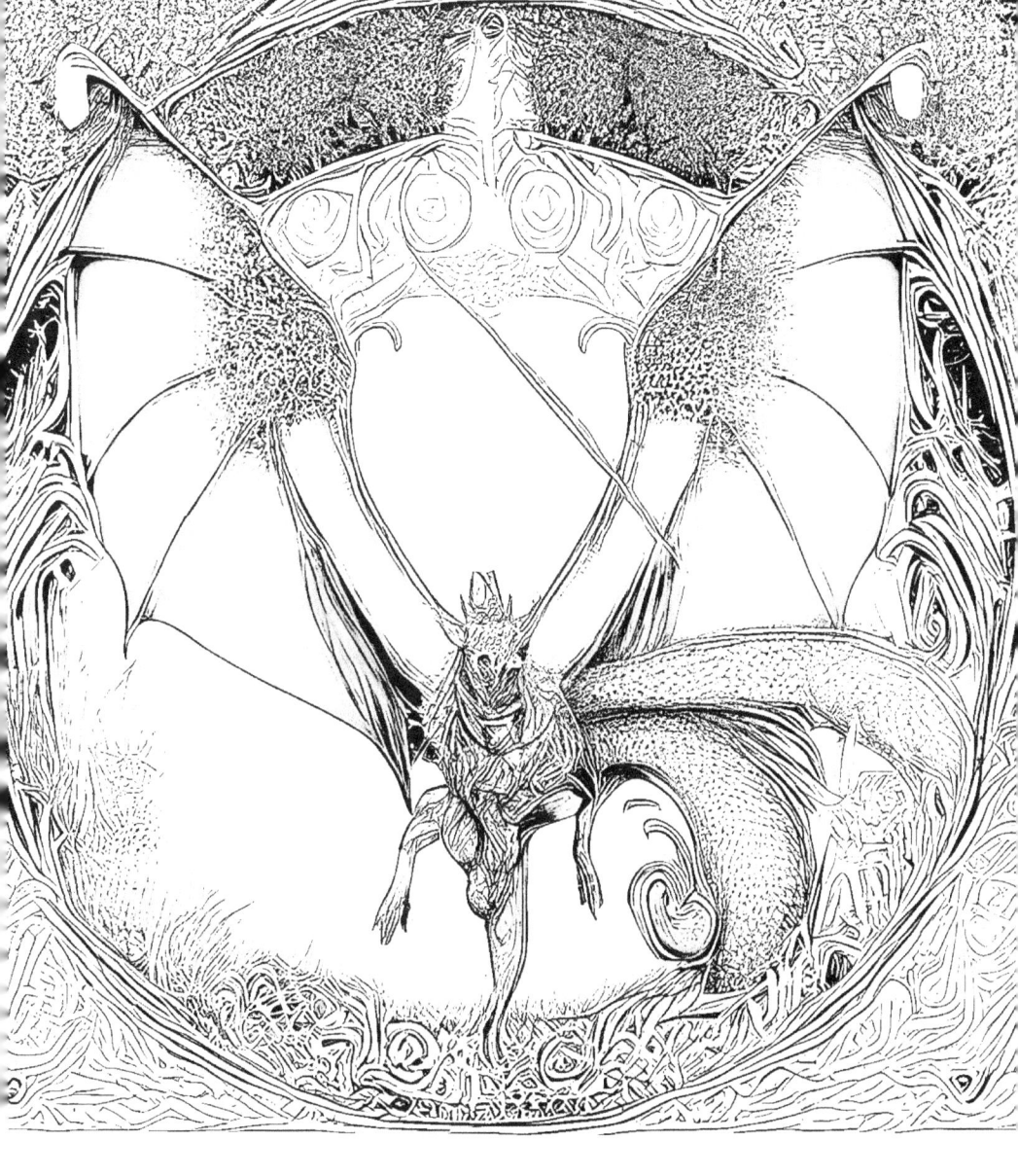

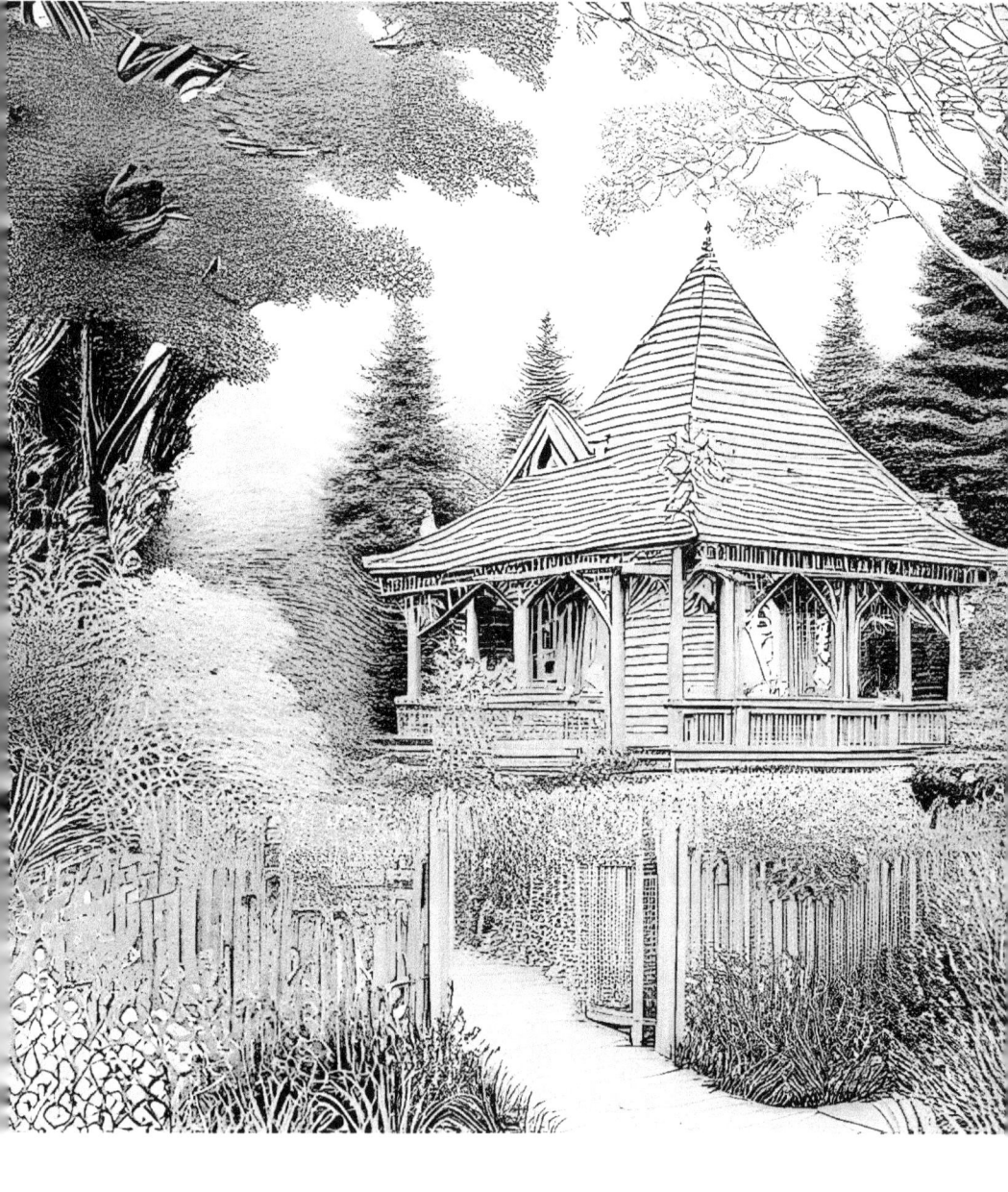

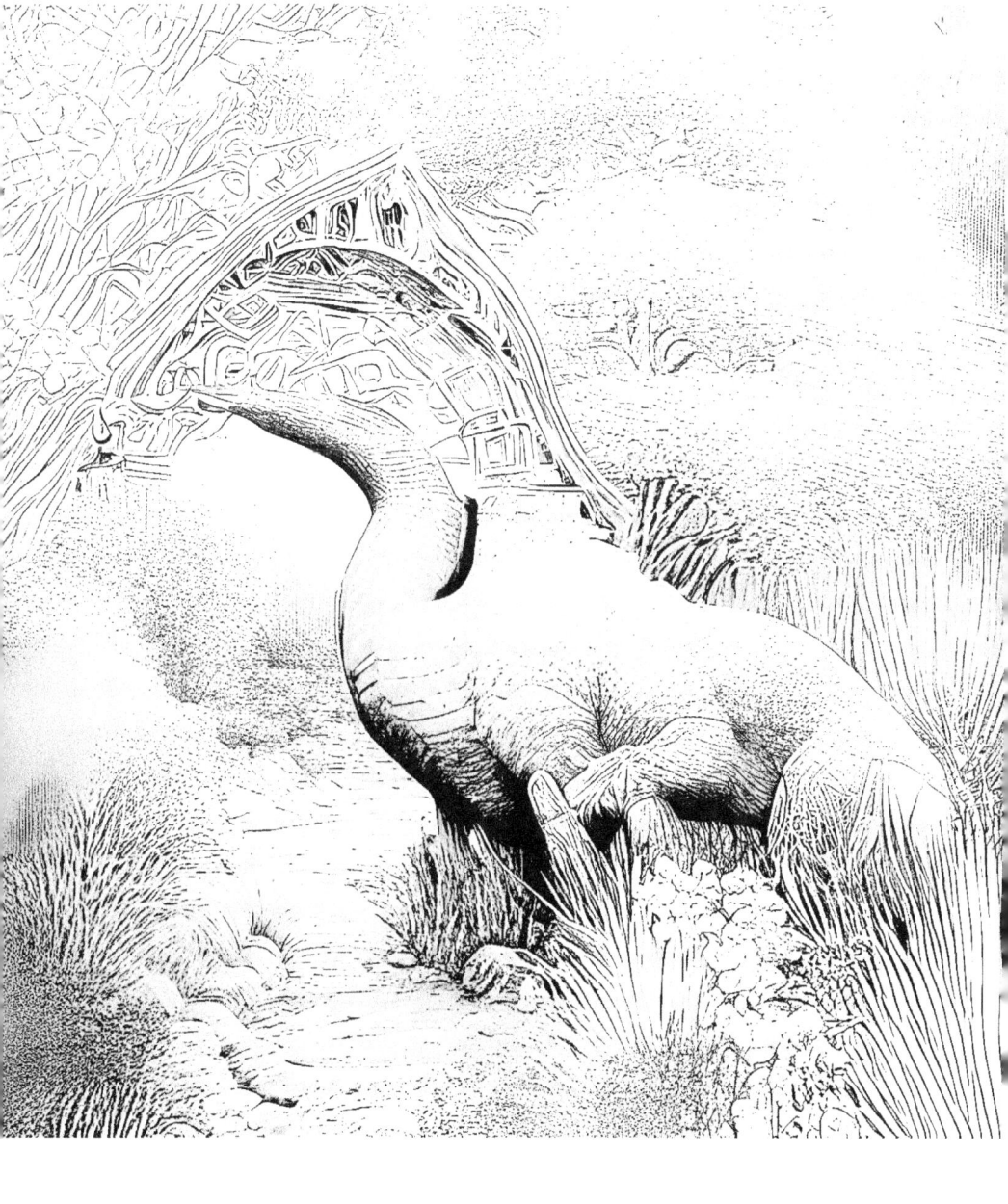

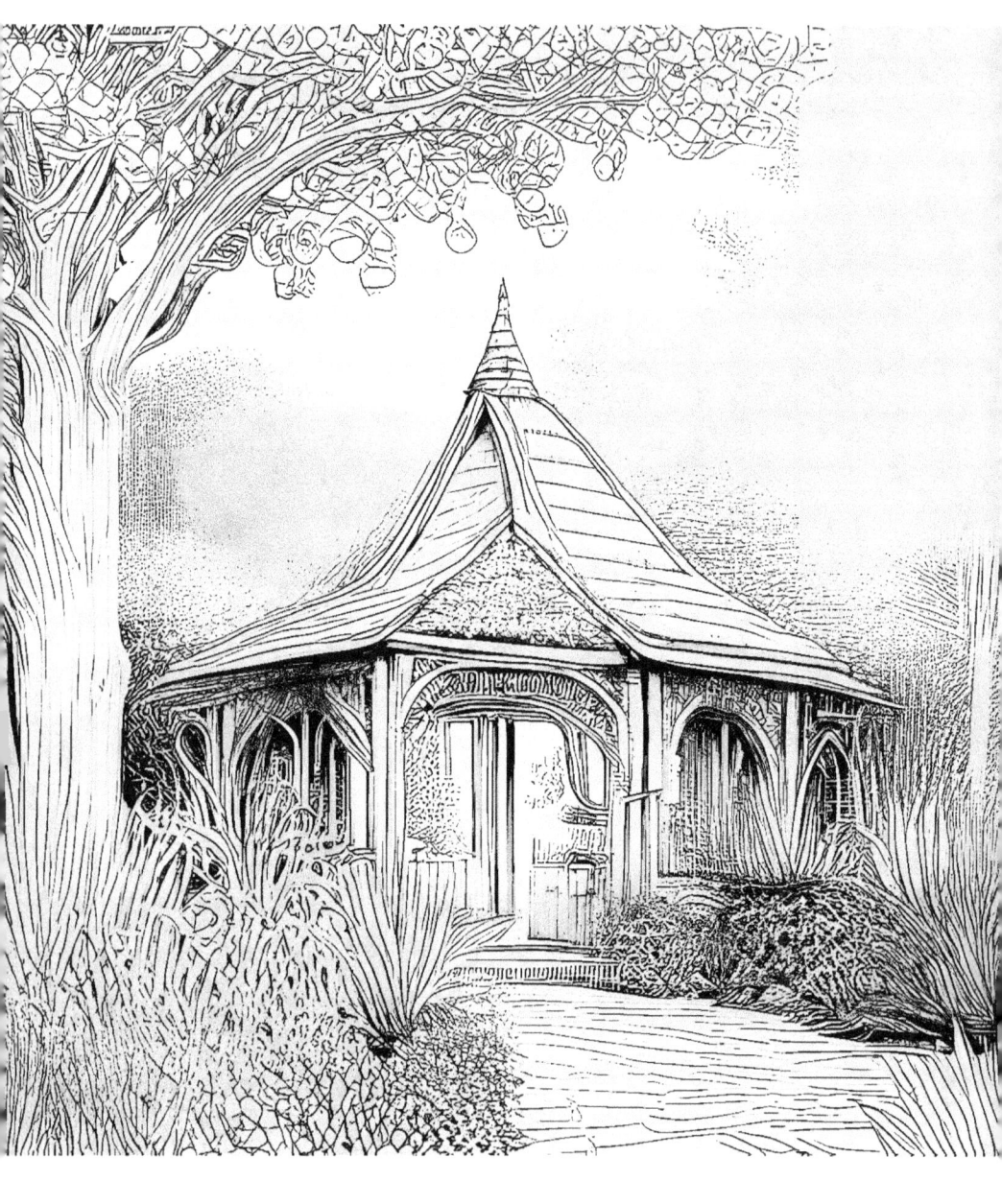

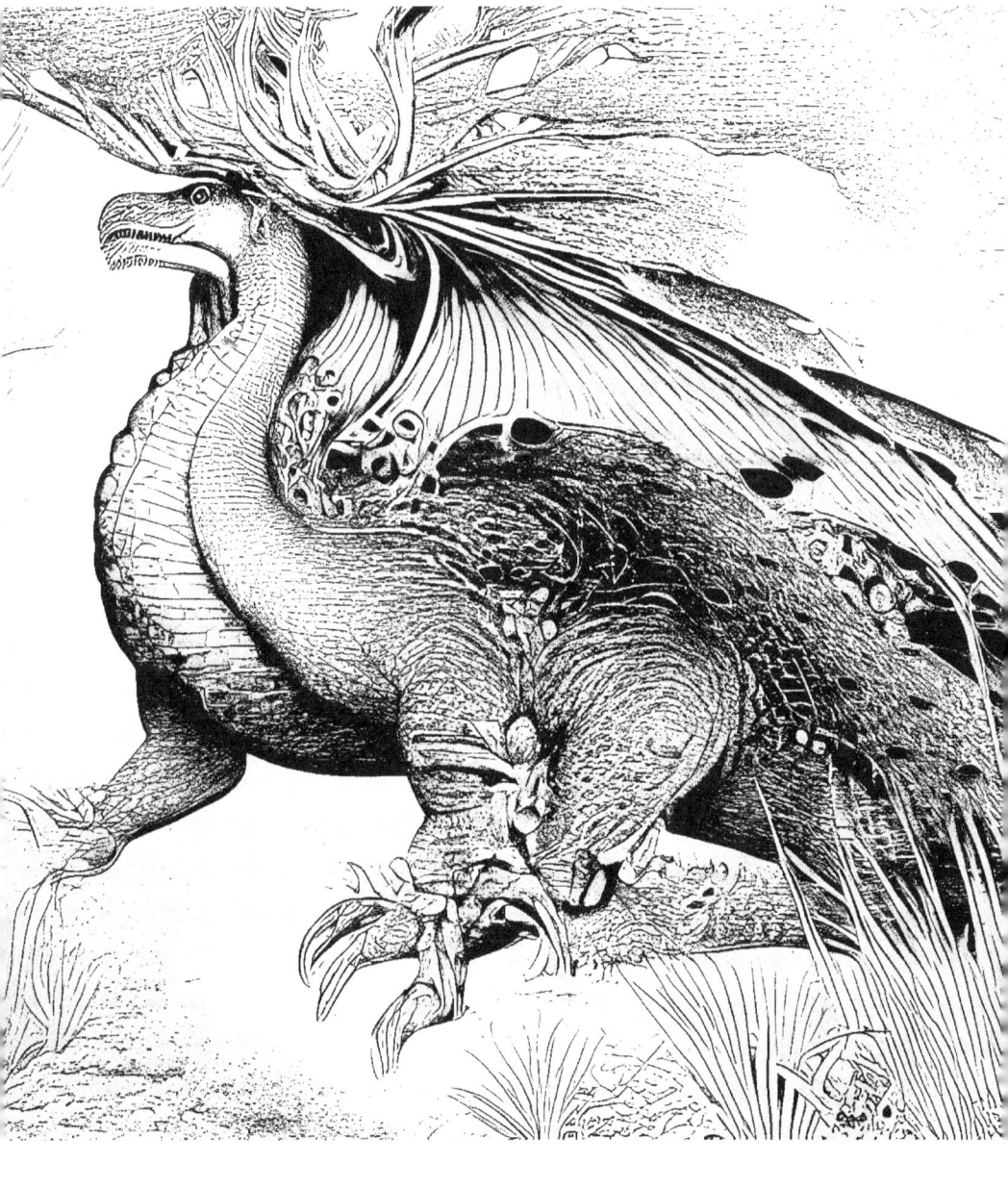

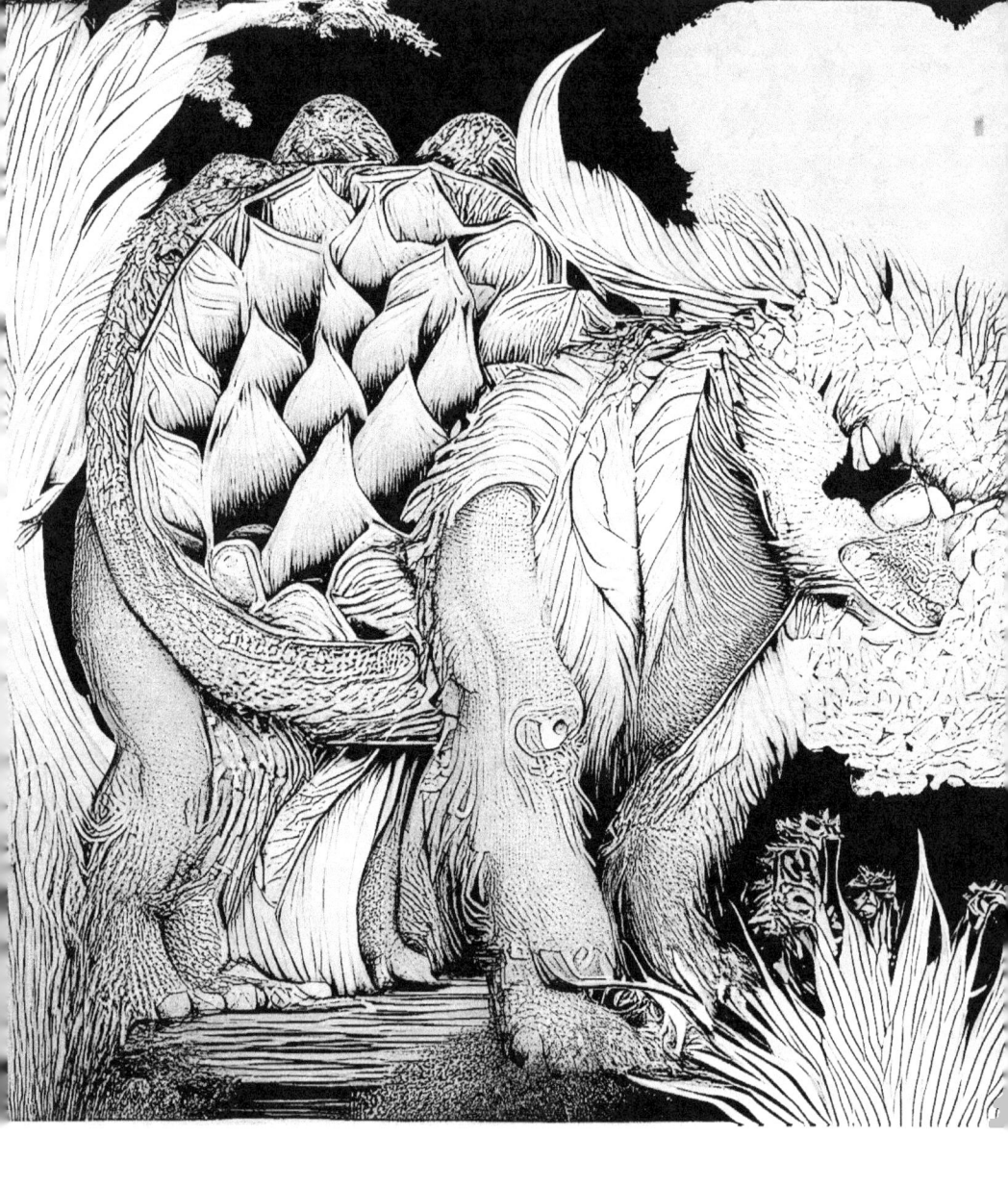

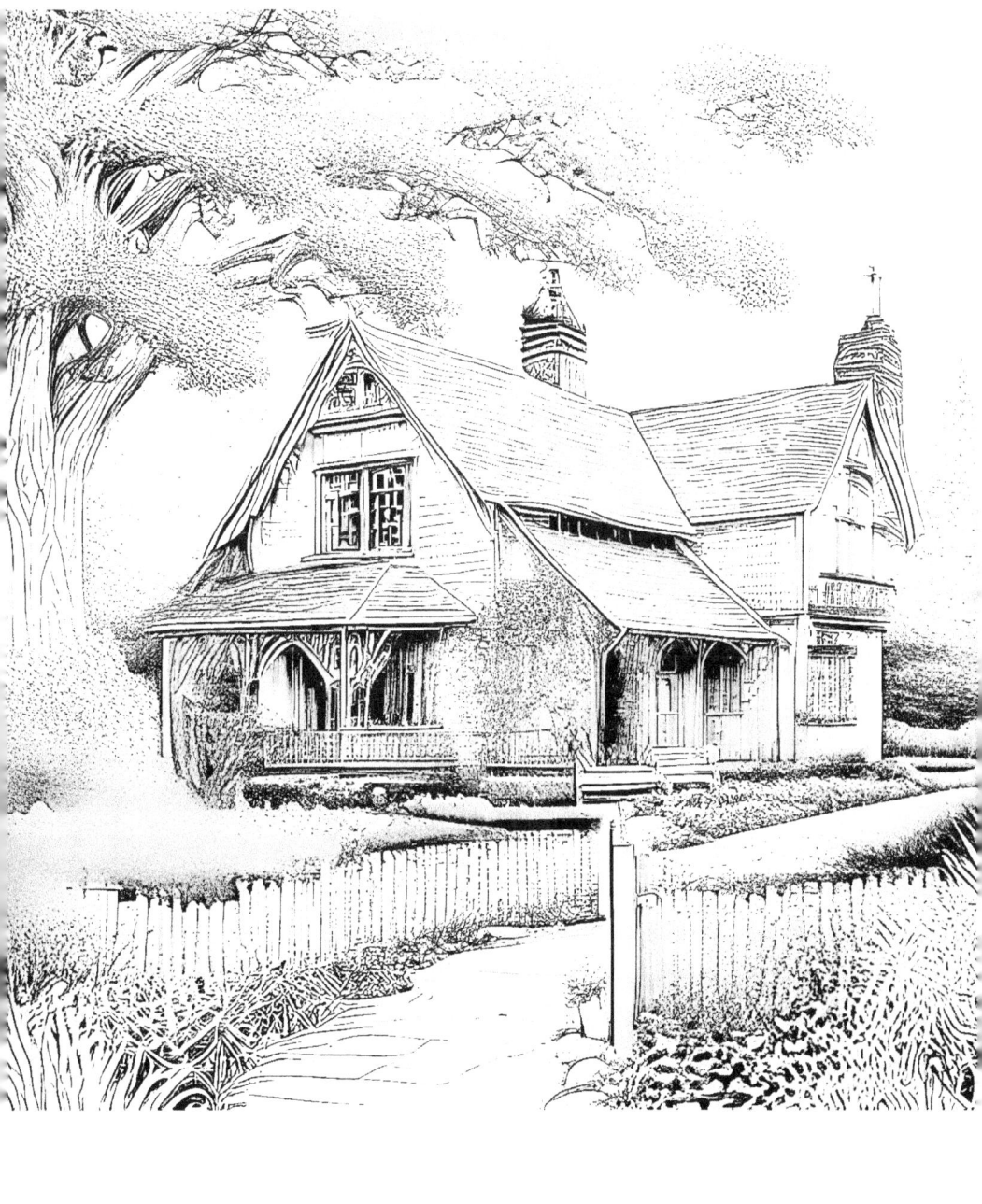

jeremyburt@ishopdailyonline.com jburt_01@hotmail.com
Make Money Online: https://ishopdailyonline.com
Print On Demand: https://ishopdaily.redbubble.com
Print On Demand @ Etsy: https://ishopdailyonline.etsy.com
dj12mind Instrumental Music Albums: https://dj12mind.com
Affiliate Products: https://index.ishopdailyonline.com
Patreon: https://www.patreon.com/user?u=80194438
Facebook: https://www.facebook.com/jeremy.burt2
Youtube:
https://www.youtube.com/channel/UCwV3nApPDh3dNHUGIX4w5nA
tiktok: https://www.tiktok.com/@jeremyburt4?lang=en
amazon: https://www.amazon.com/author/jeremyburt

THANK YOU FOR CHECKING IT OUT!

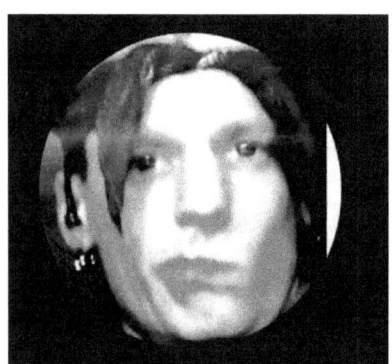

www.ingramcontent.com/pod-product-compliance
Lightning Source LLC
Chambersburg PA
CBHW072239230526
45466CB00025B/2188